IS-103: Geospatial Information Systems Specialist

By

Fema

10/31/2013

Lesson 1: Course Introduction and Position Overview

Course Overview

The Geospatial Information System (GIS) Specialist is a key GIS Unit position within the Planning Section. This course helps trainees prepare to perform the responsibilities of the GIS Specialist in a FEMA environment in response to an incident.

By the end of this course, you will be able to:

- Recognize how a GIS Specialist supports a response and recovery operation.
- Identify sources of information and data within FEMA and the emergency management community
- List the types of products commonly produced by the GIS Unit during an incident
- Identify best practices for establishing and maintaining data flow, creating products, and meeting timelines during an incident
- Identify how to appropriately handle and protect licensed, sensitive, or personal data
- Recognize how to use remote sensing products

This course will take approximately 2 hours to complete.

Lesson Overview

You can now navigate through this course. The rest of this lesson will focus on the FEMA Position Task Book (PTB) and the defined behaviors for the GIS Specialist position.

This lesson should take approximately 10 minutes to complete.

Learning Objectives

By the end of this lesson, you will be able to:

- Recognize the FEMA Qualification System (FQS) process.
- Recognize the role of the FEMA PTB in the FQS process.
- Identify the behaviors and tasks defined in the FEMA PTB for the GIS Specialist position.

FEMA PTB for GIS Specialist

This lesson aligns with the following PTB Behavior/Activity:

- Ensure readiness for assignment prior to deployment.

FEMA Qualification System (FQS)

The FQS establishes the system for qualification and certification of the FEMA workforce through experience, training, and demonstrated performance. The system was developed to:

- Ensure a qualified workforce based on performance standards,
- Establish minimum, consistent, and fair qualification requirements for all workforce positions regardless of employment status, and

- Strengthen the training and qualification standards for all workforce positions by implementing improvements based on analysis.

The steps of the FQS process are:

Step 1: The process starts when a Certifying Official issues a Position Task Book (PTB) to an individual with required FQS experience.

Step 2: After the individual completes required training and demonstrates the ability to perform all required tasks, he/she is deployable as a Trainee.

Step 3: The certification process includes review and approval. Individuals who qualify are designated as "Qualified" by the certifying authority.

Trainee/Meets Required FQS Experience/PTB Issued Area:

A performance-based qualification system is appropriate for FEMA. The FQS builds upon previous agency credentialing efforts, such as using previous task books, as the foundation to develop more robust capabilities within incident management and incident support PTBs. As a first step, individuals with the required experience are issued a PTB after the certifying official validates a candidate's experience against FWS requirements. With the issuance of the PTB, the individual becomes a "Trainee" and is eligible for deployment in that position, as a trainee.

Required Training/Demonstrated Performance Area/PTB and Training Complete Area:

Trainees engage in a cycle of completing required training (per the FEMA Qualification Sheet) and demonstrating performance of tasks outlined in the PTB at incidents. This is an iterative process, and will likely involve more than one deployment as a trainee to demonstrate performance of all position tasks. When the trainee has demonstrated performance of all position tasks and the PTB is completed, then the individual may begin the certification process.

Certification Process Review and Approval Area:

Certification is the process by which the certifying official formally validates, approves, and documents the fact that an individual is qualified for a specific FQS position. The certifying official considers a number of factors including the variety of incidents (e.g., floods, tornados, hurricanes. etc.); their size and complexity; and the number of assignments for each individual.

"Qualified"/Qualification Issued Area:

When the certifying official approves an individual for certification, the trainee is determined to be qualified for the target position and receives a qualification letter indicating that his/her status has been changed from "trainee" to "qualified."

FEMA PTB for GIS Specialist
The GIS Specialist PTB contains all the critical behaviors, activities, and tasks required to become certified as a GIS Specialist. When a trainee successfully demonstrates task performance for an FQS evaluator at an incident, the Evaluator signs off on those tasks in the trainee's PTB. The PTB serves as the official record of successfully completed tasks. This course does not address all of the behaviors and tasks in the PTB because many of the more generic behaviors, such as following established safety and security procedures, are addressed in other required FEMA training.

Additional Training That Supports the Development of GIS Knowledge and Skills

Additional training designed to develop GIS knowledge and skills includes:
- Introduction to GIS courses (provided by many external sources)
- EMI (E190) ArcGIS for Emergency Managers
- ESRI – Learning ArcGIS Desktop
- ESRI – HAZUS-MH online courses
- ESRI – Learning ArcGIS Spatial Analyst
- ESRI – Creating, Editing and Managing Geodatabases for ArcGIS Desktop
- ESRI – Understanding GIS Queries
- ESRI – Using Python in ArcGIS Desktop – Introduction to Python and Integration with ArcGIS Deskto
- ESRI – Basics of the Geodatabase Data Model

Lesson Summary

This lesson presented the following topics:
- The FQS Process
- The Role of the PTB in the FQS
- FEMA's GIS Specialist PTB

The next lesson presents information about the resources you will use and the processes you will follow as a GISP at an incident, and describes how the GIS Unit interacts with and supports the incident response and recovery operation.

Lesson 2: Identifying Resources and Processes

Lesson Overview

Lesson 2 provides information about the resources and processes you will use as a GISP. It reviews different components of the ICS organization and the GIS unit, identifies key GIS doctrine, and identifies various GIS systems, tools, and data sources.

This lesson should take approximately 15 minutes to complete.

Learning Objectives

By the end of this lesson, you will be able to:

- Recognize how GIS supports other components in a JFO
- Identify key GIS doctrine and materials
- Identify FEMA GIS systems and tools
- Recognize authoritative data sources

Tying It Back to the Job

This lesson aligns with the following PTB Behavior/Activity:

- Ensure readiness for assignment prior to deployment.

Incident Command System Structure

As a new GISP, one of your first items of business is get a sense of how the organization is structured and find out who you'll be working with. This lesson will help you do that.

Let's start with an overview of the incident management structure you'll be working within.

All FEMA incident management activities are organized according to the Incident Command System (ICS) structure. Under the leadership of the Unified Coordination Group (UCG), a FEMA Joint Field Office (JFO) includes the following four Sections: Operations, Planning, Logistics, and Finance & Administration. The Geospatial Information Unit (GIU) is organized within the Planning Section.

Joint Field Office

The Joint Field Office (JFO) is the primary Federal incident management field structure. It is a temporary Federal facility established to provide a central point for Federal, State, tribal, and local governments and private sector and nongovernmental organizations with responsibility for incident oversight, directions, and/or assistance to effectively coordinate and direct prevention, preparedness, response, and recovery actions. Typically, the JFO is located at or near the incident area of operations.

Unified Coordination Group (UCG)
The Unified Coordination Group (UCG) at the incident has the primary responsibility to manage the incident. All other levels of the FEMA Chain of Command support the UCG. The UCG is comprised, at a minimum, of the Federal Coordinating Officer (FCO) and State Coordinating Officer (SCO) and any and all major stakeholders such as Tribal governments, Local jurisdictions, or the private sector.

Operations Section
The Operations Section is responsible for all tactical incident operations and implementation of the Incident Action Plan (IAP). The Operations Section coordinates operational support with on-scene incident management efforts and supervises the resources needed to accomplish incident objectives.

Planning Section
The Planning Section is responsible for the collection, evaluation, and dissemination of operational information related to the incident, and for the preparation and documentation of the Incident Action Plan (IAP), functional plans, Advanced Operational Plans (AOPs), strategic plans, and Situation Reports. The Planning Section also maintains information on the current and forecasted situation and reports on the status of resources assigned to the incident. The Planning Section prepares and documents Federal support actions and develops a number of plans.

Geospatial Information Unit
The Geospatial Information Unit (GIU) is responsible for producing all incident specific geospatial products (such as maps, reports, and GIS data). The GIU works closely with other units in the Planning Section to develop the products that are needed to support all phases of the incident (prevention, protection, mitigation, response and recovery).
The use of GIS products and analysis helps provide context for decision makers and gives them a clearer picture of what is occurring at the incident level (i.e., better situational awareness of the incident).

Logistics Section
The Logistics Section is responsible for providing facilities, services, and materials for the incident. This section also orders resources and develops the Transportation, Communications, and Medical Plans.

Finance & Administration Section
The Finance / Administration Section is responsible for all administrative and financial considerations surrounding an incident, including: financial management, monitoring, and tracking of all Federal costs relating to the incident and the functioning of the JFO.

GIU Mission and Responsibilities

As a new GIS Specialist, it's also important to be familiar with your Unit's mission and responsibilities.

What is the Mission of the GIU?

The mission of the GIU is to produce high-quality geospatial products, data and services in support of emergency management. Geospatial products and information play a key role in FEMA's preparation for and response to incidents.

What are the Responsibilities of the GIU?

GIU responsibilities include the following:

- Generating geospatial products
- Managing geospatial data
- Ensuring compliance with established policies and protocols
- Providing geospatial coordination and customer service
- Operating specialized hardware and software applications

GIU Positions

Now let's take a look at the staff members within the GIU.

Who Staffs the GIU?

For a large-scale incident, the leader of the GIU at the JFO is generally the Geospatial Information Unit Leader (GIUL) who reports directly to the Planning Section Chief. In smaller disasters, the Unit may be led by a Geospatial Information Manager (GIMG). The GIUL/GIMG is supported by one or more Geospatial Information System Specialists (GISPs), and, when needed, Remote Sensing Specialists (RMSPs) as well.

While the GIU organizational structure is flexible, each position has a specific set of responsibilities which support organizational efficiency as well as unity of command.

Geospatial Information Unit Leader (GIUL)

- Supervises GIMGs, GISPs, and RMSPs, within his/her span of control
- Participates in intra-agency and multi-agency geospatial coordination with State, FEMA and NRF partners involved in geospatial activities
- Responsible for standing up and demobilizing the GIU
- Participates in the Incident Action Planning process

Geospatial Information Manager (GIMG)
- Reports to the GIUL
- Coordinates GIS requirements and supervises assigned GISP
- Prioritizes GIS production and activities within assigned area of responsibility
- Works with product requestors to properly define requirements and ensures the timely preparation and delivery of recurring and ad hoc GIS products
- Participates in the Incident Action Planning process

Geospatial Information Systems Specialist (GISP)
- Reports to the GIMG
- Collects data from internal and external stakeholders to develop and update geospatial products
- Integrate event-specific model output in coordination with authoritative sources
- Develop key geospatial products
- Participates in the Incident Action Planning process

Remote Sensing Specialist (RMSP)
- Responsible for the coordination of RS requirements, resources, and requests for the team
- Operates as task originator and collection manager for assets related to the operation
- Works with GIMGs to ensure imagery-derived products are delivered in a timely manner

GIS Support for Other Components of the JFO

As a GIS Specialist, you may be asked to provide products and services for a variety of different components within the JFO, such as:
- Unified Coordination Group (UCG)
- Operations Section
- Planning Section
- Logistics Section
- Finance & Administration Section
- Command Staff, including External Affairs

Unified Coordination Group (UCG)

A GISP may provide high level information for decision makers, such as impacted area or status of critical infrastructure or grant programs.

Operations Section
A GISP generally provides the most support to the Operations Section, including the production of products related to the grant programs or environmental impacts, response to the impacts of the incident to households and infrastructure, or other, specialized support, such as to Search and Rescue teams.

Planning Section
A GISP often supports the Planning Section's situational awareness responsibilities, incident action planning, and may also support resource tracking and provide visualizations.

Logistics Section
A GISP may provide support to facility layout and management, or to points of distribution.

Finance & Administration Section
A GISP may provide information to support disaster cost estimation process, or maps of the local commuting area circumference to provide information for disaster administration policies.

Command Staff, including External Affairs
A GISP may provide products related to External Affairs, including the Community Relations staff or to support requests from Congressional staffers. A GISP may also provide support to the Safety Officer, Chief of Staff or other Command Staff positions.

GIU Positions

As a GISP, it is important to be familiar with the doctrine that guides your work. Critical GIS doctrine is provided in the following documents. Taking the time to become familiar with the information in these documents will make the transition into a GIU much smoother.

Federal Interagency Geospatial Concept of Operations (GeoCONOPS)

- Documents current geospatial practice support the NRF and Stafford Act activities
- Identifies and aligns the geospatial resources required to support the Whole Community, NRF, ESF, and supporting Federal mission partners
- Intended to reduce redundancy and confusion and ensure efficient access to geospatial information for incident management

Geospatial Incident Management and Support Guide

- Provides an overview of National/Regional Incident Support positions as well as Incident-level positions during event response/recovery
- Describes how these positions work with each other during an incident

GIS Systems

When you check-in to a JFO, you will receive a laptop that includes all the software you need to perform your assigned duties. This will include standard GIS tools and software available to FEMA personnel.

In addition to the laptop, you will be given access to geospatial data, as well as access to the printers (including desk printers and large-format printers) you may need to produce your products.

For additional information about FEMA GIS enterprise tools, see the Geospatial Incident Management and Support Guide.

GIS Data Sources

As a GISP, one of your primary responsibilities will be to gather the data needed to complete your tasks. You will have a number of different data sources at your disposal as you do so.

Foundation-Level Data

Foundation-Level Data is a compilation of geospatial data layers characterizing domestic infrastructure, boundaries and other information for emergency preparedness, response and recovery communities.

Examples of foundation-level data sources include:

Homeland Security Infrastructure Program (HSIP) provides inclusive national dataset of integrated views of national infrastructure and critical asset information.

The **USGS National Map** is a collaborative effort of the United States Geological Survey (USGS) and other federal, state, and local agencies to improve and deliver topographic information for the United States. It provides "...a seamless, continuously maintained set of public domain geographic base information that will serve as a foundation for integrating, sharing, and using other data easily and consistently".

geodata.gov is an Internet-based capability that provides shared and trusted geospatial data, services, and applications for use by government agencies and partners.

State and Local Data

State and local data is a compilation of geospatial data layers characterizing domestic infrastructure, boundaries and other information produced by State and local government organizations. Sometimes data produced by State and local organizations is more accurate than Federally produced data.

Examples of State and local data sources include:
State Geospatial Departments which provide clearinghouses and central repositories for spatial data.
The **National States Geographic Information Council** (NSGIC) has created a tool for states and their partners, whose primary purpose is to track the status of GIS in use by state and local governments to aid the planning and building of Spatial Data Infrastructures. This tool is Ramona (also referred to as the GIS Inventory).

Incident-Specific Data
Incident-Specific Data is data unique to the event. Often this valuable information is the most accurate data for the incident, but communication of data can be difficult throughout organizational levels during response and recovery.
Examples of incident-specific data sources include:
Volunteered Geographic Information (VGI), the harnessing tools to create, assemble, and disseminate geographic data provided voluntarily by individuals.
FEMA data, including grant program data (Individual Assistance applicants, Public Assistance Project Worksheets, Mitigation grant locations); damaged area data, status of declarations and preliminary damage assessments, Federal teams and resources.
State data, including power status and damaged area data, State teams and resources.
Local data, including damaged area data, local teams and resources.

Recognizing Authoritative Data Sources
When collecting information, you have many possible sources to work with. While all information is valuable for establishing Situational Awareness, it is important to ensure that information is cross-checked with an authoritative data source.

What is an Authoritative Data Source?
An authoritative data source is a recognized or official data production source with a designated mission statement or source/product to publish reliable and accurate data for subsequent use.
Authoritative data falls into one of two categories:
- Rational Authority
- Expert Authority

Rational Authority
Rational Authority - Government agencies are by default the "authoritative" sources for data or services that they produce or have statutory responsibility for.
Examples of rational authorities include:
- USGS - Streams and river data
- USGS – National Elevation Datasets
- FEMA – FEMA Regional Offices
- FEMA - Hurricane Evacuation Routes

Expert Authority

Expert (scientifically) authoritative data is defined in terms of the various professions under which the standards and methodology for data are created.

Examples of expert authority include:

- Volunteered Geographic Information (VGI) such as imagery and information analysis
- Data and analysis provided by academia
- Studies conducted by recognized think tanks

Data sources can be either internal or external to the JFO.

Internal

Sources within the JFO include: FEMA, Emergency Support Functions (ESFs), State counterparts

External

External sources with the emergency management community include: FEMA Regional and national staff, Public/Private Utility providers such as ConEdison, Waste Management, etc.

Credible and Non-Credible Sources

Being able to quickly gather data that is both current and accurate is always a challenge. You will need to continuously evaluate your data sources since some will be more credible than others.

Credible Sources

A credible source is a source that offers "reasonable grounds for being believed." It is important to establish a list of trusted, credible sources from which to obtain data to support geospatial production. While not considered "authoritative," this mix of open sources, as well as official information providers should become a go-to constellation of data resources for geospatial data collection and exploitation within FEMA.

Non-Credible Sources

Sources that lack credibility should rarely be used, if ever, within FEMA official production and reporting; however, there will be certain occasions where the only source reporting a specific piece of data that fulfills an information gap will make its way into a product. Such data should always be caveated within the product, and, as soon as practical, follow-up research should be conducted to determine the validity of that specific piece of data.

Lesson Summary

This lesson presented the following topics:

- Recognize how GIS supports other components in a JFO
- Identify key GIS doctrine and materials
- Identify FEMA GIS systems and tools
- Recognize authoritative data sources

The next lesson explains how to get started in a JFO.

Lesson 3: Getting Started

Lesson Overview

In the previous lesson you were introduced to the resources and processes you will use on the job. In order to be an effective GIS Specialist, you need to know how to set up in your new environment and use the tools and resources you will have access to.

This lesson highlights the initial actions you should take upon entering the JFO and provides an overview of the kinds of GIS products you will be expected to produce.

This lesson should take approximately 15 minutes to complete.

Learning Objectives

By the end of this lesson, you will be able to:

- Recognize how to check in to a Joint Field Office
- Identify how to gather information relevant to an assignment
- Identify the types of GIS products that need to be produced during a disaster

Tying It Back to the Job

This lesson aligns with the following PTB Behaviors/Activities:

- Ensure readiness for assignment prior to deployment.
- Follow proper check-in procedures upon arrival and obtain job-required equipment and supplies.
- Obtain an initial briefing from immediate supervisor and gather information relevant to your assignment.

Checking in to the Joint Field Office

Every member of the FEMA team must check in to the Joint Field Office (JFO) upon arrival to obtain necessary equipment and supplies and ensure the right procedures are being followed. Check in procedures include:

- Checking in with your supervisor
- Completing a check in packet
- Obtaining agency identification
- Checking in with the Accountable Property Manager (APM)
- Checking in with the Automated Deployment Database (ADD)
- Filling out a JFO IT Help Desk request form
- Completing security training if applicable

Obtaining agency identification

This may be a badge or another type of government-issued identification issued to FEMA staff as applicable.

Checking in with the Accountable Property Manager

You will need to check in with the Accountable Property Manager (APM) in order to obtain the additional job-required supplies or equipment you will need, such as:

- Laptop with the specialized GIS hardware and software you will need
- Cellular or desk phone

- Handheld GPS (if applicable)
- Camera (if applicable)
- Office supplies
- Maps
- Air Card (if applicable)

Check in with the Automated Deployment Database (ADD)

To check in to with the Automated Deployment Database (ADD), you will need the following information:

- Social Security Number
- Disaster Number
- Lodging phone number and address
- Rental car information
- Emergency contact information

Filling out a JFO IT Help Desk

You will need to fill out a JFO IT Help Desk request form before your laptop can be mapped to the JFO servers, printers, and other electronic equipment you may need to do your work.

Obtaining an Initial Briefing

After you have checked in to the JFO and gathered the necessary supplies, the next step is to obtain an initial briefing. Your immediate supervisor's briefing should provide you with:

- Administrative documentation and procedures
- Initial direction about your assignment
- Situational information relevant to your tasks
- Information about where/how data is being stored
- Production standards for the operation

During the initial briefing, you should bring up any topics, issues, or concerns you may have about your assignment.

Administrative documentation and procedures

Your supervisor should provide you with the following:

- Information on how to check into the Automated Deployment Database (ADD)
- Copy of ICS 205A (Communications List), the call-down list for the Unit
- Tour of the key areas and the facility and introduce you to the PSC and Unit Lead
- Establish communication with your assigned FEMA Qualification System Coach and Evaluator
- Information on product schedule and expected work hours

Where and how data is stored

As this varies from site to site and event to event, be sure to see your supervisor for more information.

Production standards for the operation
It is essential that consistency be maintained throughout the Unit for all geospatial products. Following prescribed standards helps minimize confusion and allows for a more efficient response.

Maintain consistency for the following elements for all GIS products:

- **Symbology** – labeling, terms used, etc.
- **Product updates** – updating progress, marking tasks as completed, etc.
- **Product layout** – templates, style guides, etc.

Data Sources

In order to begin working on an assignment, you must know where to find the data and how to work with sources.

As you learned in Lesson 2, there are a number of data sources which you can use to collect data: internal and external partners, news sources, etc.

It is your job to identify data sources for the information you need.

Data Sources
Refer to Lesson 2 for a listing of available data sources for each of the following three categories:

- Foundation-Level data
- State and Local Data
- Incident-Specific Data

Collecting Data

Data is required for every geospatial product and the quality of the data collected impacts the overall value of the products produced. When collecting data, there are a number of considerations to keep in mind.

You should:

- Make sure data and metadata is accurate and current.
- Follow established data and metadata management standards.
- Properly protect licensed or sensitive data.
- Work closely with internal and external partners.

You will learn more about protecting sensitive data in Lesson 6.

Ensure that your data and metadata is accurate and current
As you learned in Lesson 2, although information can come from any number of sources, it is essential that you ensure that all information that you are collecting is cross-checked with authoritative data sources. This will ensure that the GIS products that are accurate and reliable.

In addition, you should always ensure that GIS products are consistently updated with current information.

Follow established data and metadata management standards

Anyone who has worked in a busy GIU supporting a large disaster knows that without some basic rules and standards, file shares and databases can quickly become an intractable realm of chaos. GIS offices usually require detailed documentation (metadata) and careful organization of data, but when deliverables are required twice daily, current to the hour, or when lives may be on the line, it is easy for disciplined focus on metadata to be lost and duplication of data and effort increase exponentially.

At minimum, metadata should include information on who created the data, when it was created, and a brief attribution description.

Strategies for addressing this challenge have been established. You should check with your supervisor to make sure you understand what standards you should follow.

Properly protect licensed or sensitive data from data sources

You should ensure that all sensitive material is marked as such and is properly secured. You will learn more about protecting sensitive data in Lesson 6.

Work closely with internal and external partners

As you learned in the previous lesson, information comes from a variety of sources, including interaction with others. In order to achieve greater situational awareness, you will want to maintain strong relationships with other agencies and individuals. This will help facilitate effective data sharing and ensure that everyone has a shared understanding of the incident.

GIS Products and Functional Areas

The types of services and products you will be asked to produce will vary depending on the functional area you are working within.

Based on your interests, experiences, and skills, you may be assigned to work with any of the following functional areas:

- Operations Section
- Emergency Services Branch
- External Affairs
- Hazard Mitigation Branch
- Individual Assistance Branch
- Logistics Section
- Long-Term Community Recovery Branch
- Planning Section
- Public Assistance / Infrastructure Branch

Operations Section

- A GISP may provide high level information for decision makers, such as impacted area or status of critical infrastructure or grant programs.

Emergency Services Branch
- Provides critical support for meeting the Emergency Services Branch requirements, such as public health and medical or search and rescue activities

External Affairs
- Supports Community Relations, Public Information and External Affairs and Congressional Affairs
- Outreach products for the public (e.g. data distributions for public release,) will be coordinated from this team

Hazard Mitigation Branch
- Coordinates with subject matter experts (SMEs) and disciplinary experts for authoritative data and models to define incident areas
- Areas include NFIP, Floodplain, and the development of depth grids, SLOSH, etc.

Logistics Section
- A GISP may provide high level information for decision makers, such as impacted area or status of critical infrastructure or grant programs.

Individual Assistance Branch
- Supports Evacuations, Mass Care, Sheltering Individual Assistance, Direct Housing Programs and Voluntary Agencies (VOLAGs)
- Main products rely on data from the FEMA reports server for Individual Assistance registrations
- Special emphasis on tracking displaced populations is important for Response

Long-Term Community Recovery Branch
- Focuses on damages and resources in housing, infrastructure/environment, and economy sectors
- Aims to re-establish a healthy, functioning community that will sustain itself over time

Planning Section
- Supports special projects, senior executive summary products and high-priority project requests, and special geographic reference products
- The Planning Section support lead will develop prototype projects for cyclic map requests used in daily Executive Briefings
- The Planning Specialist will integrate web map services for FEMA's situational awareness tools

Public Assistance / Infrastructure Branch
- Supports Infrastructure, Power, HAZMAT/Environmental Special Considerations and Debris mission
- Projects from ESF-3 and ESF-12 missions occur most frequently in Response

- Subject matter expertise in natural sciences as well as experience in civil engineering recommended

Types of GIS Requests

In a large event, it is not uncommon for the GIU to support large numbers of simultaneous projects per Operational Period. As you just learned, the specific types of services and products you will be asked to provide depends on the functional area you work within, the type of disaster you are supporting, and the operational tempo.

In general, however, you will find that GIU production generally supports three types of GIS requests:
- Cyclic products at daily or operational period update cycles
- Intermittently updated products
- Ad hoc products

Cyclic products at daily or operational period update cycles

Cyclic products are during every operational period and are used during periods of operational activity that require constant shared situational awareness. They are usually required for every disaster and are often used within Executive Briefings. Cyclic products are the best candidates for integration with interactive web mapping through FEMA's situational awareness tools. They require a large amount of initial coordination to develop data and templates, and then they are updated regularly with little further development throughout the disaster. There may be a large number of these projects in the early stages of Response and Recovery, requiring significant resources to support.

Intermittently updated products

Intermittently updated products involve activity that is constant, though irregular. Map updates involve source data and formats that may be relatively unchanging, but require intermittent coordination for new revisions and updates. Some examples include the Declarations status map, and Damage Assessment maps. These projects require more coordination on the Geospatial unit side, as they are often the most common and can often 'evolve' and change as a mission support area progresses from Response to Recovery.

Ad hoc products

Ad hoc products will not require many revisions, and are designed for decision support, or unique issues which will change or be resolved. These are often 'one-time' projects which may involve significant focus for a short amount of time, and often have limited distribution. Alternatively, they may be reference products based on static information such as demographic or geographic data that are developed once.

Lesson Summary

This lesson presented the following topics:

- Recognize how to check in to a Joint Field Office
- Identify how to gather information relevant to an assignment
- Identify the types of GIS products that need to be produced during a disaster

The next lesson explains how to respond to common requests for GIS services and products.

Lesson 4: Responding to Common Requests

Lesson Overview

In Lesson 3, you learned how to get set up for your work as a GIS specialist. This lesson presents information about the GIS products you will be asked to produce and provides an overview of the workflow process you will follow as you produce these products. It also provides an overview of the quality assurance/ quality control process used to ensure the production of high quality GIS products.

This lesson should take approximately 15 minutes to complete.

Learning Objectives

By the end of this lesson, you will be able to:

- Identify the GIS products commonly produced during an incident
- Recognize the GIS product workflow process
- Recognize the quality assurance/quality control process used to ensure the quality of GIS products

Tying It Back to the Job

This lesson aligns with the following PTB Behaviors/Activities:

- Manage geospatial data
- Generate geospatial products
- Comply with established policy and protocols
- Provide geospatial coordination and customer service

Key GIS Products During a Disaster

As you learned in Lesson 3, the products produced during a disaster will vary based on the type of disaster, the stage of the disaster, and the functional area that you are assigned to. There are, however, a number of common GIS products you may be asked to produce. These include:

- Incident-specific maps
- Reference maps
- Quantitative/qualitative thematic maps
- Interactive map products

Incident-specific maps

Incident-specific mapping involves the development and production of maps that reflect real-time information that is related to the incident. This could be evacuation data or locations of responding elements and resources. This real-time information is often integrated with referential demographic or geographic information to make a product that is more operationally useful.

For example, satellite imagery derived for damage assessment data might be combined with road overlays to identify potentially problematic lines of ground transportation that could be of extreme interest to decision makers when planning field activities. Some of the more common incident-specific maps include:

- Declaration Status Maps show the counties or municipalities designated by a disaster declaration.
- Incident Area Maps are used to indicate the levels of damage, hazard specific information, and the incident area for given jurisdictional areas. This can be used for the ICS 201 form or Incident Action Plan map.
- Resource Tracking Maps are used to show the location of emergency response teams and commodities, facilities, Mobile Disaster Recovery Centers (MDRC) etc. and their current status, whether deployed, available for deployment or on rotation.
- Facility Maps – Facilities such as the location and identification of staging areas can be an important map, particularly in large scale events where large quantities of materials and supplies are being brought into the disaster areas.

Reference maps

Reference Mapping involves the production of maps graphically reflecting referential statistics or information. These could include jurisdictional boundaries, congressional districts, population demographic breakdowns, locations of residential, commercial, industrial, and governmental facilities, income and economic information, infrastructure, etc. Community Relations often requests the development of a visual demographic profile of a particular area by combining different types of information such as age and number of people living in different types of housing stock, or income and rental properties.
Some of the more common reference maps include:

- Political jurisdiction maps
- Geographic and demographic maps
- Census products
- Common critical facilities

Quantitative and qualitative thematic maps

Thematic maps are designed to communicate more abstract quantitative or qualitative observations of entities or areas within and surrounding the subject.
Individual Assistance grant applicant density grid analysis is one of the most common thematic maps. To make the results more meaningful, the applicant damaged address points may be weighted based on their grant funding amounts. This dollars-per-square-mile approach quickly identifies neighborhoods receiving the most FEMA assistance. This generalization of data is also a technique for displaying information protected under the Privacy Act of 1974 (described further in Lesson 6) without identifying individuals.

Interactive map products

Interactive maps like web mapping systems and GIS viewer clients allow users to interact directly with GIS data. Some interactive map options are available to anyone, while others require a login. Other options require data and other manipulation by the GIS Unit to be used.

FEMA has developed several web mapping viewers that allow users to view and manipulate data. These viewers display FEMA's geospatial data, as well as other agencies' data, to allow for the analysis and demonstration of operationally relevant information to be shared among multiple operation centers and teams. Other similar applications exist at the State and local level to support their emergency management efforts.

Interactive maps facilitate collaborative planning, assist in achieving shared situational awareness, and facilitate management decision-making.

Responding to Project Requests

While you have no doubt produced GIS products before, you may not be familiar with the FEMA GIS production process. At a high level, the FEMA GIS workflow process includes the following phases:

- Planning & Direction
- Project Assignment
- Exploration
- Production
- Dissemination

You will learn more about each phase throughout this lesson.

PHASE 1: Planning & Direction

The GIS production process starts with the receipt of a GIS request by the GIUL (for a large incident), or the GIMG (for a smaller incident). The request may be submitted either in hardcopy format or through a web-based system.

Once received, the GIUL/GIMG uses his/her expertise to:

- Determine the feasibility of the project request
- Verify the project request against existing products
- Determine restrictions/security issues related to the project request

The GIUL/GIMG then prioritizes the project request, identifies the best person to complete the request, and assigns the request to a GIS Specialist for completion.

Determine the feasibility of the project request

Not all product requests may be feasible given resource capacity, existing projects, and the timeline. The GIUL/GIMG has to weigh the feasibility of the project request and decide whether it should be taken up.

Verify the project request against existing products

The GIUL/GIMG has to determine whether the project request overlaps with an existing request. If so, it would save resources to modify or copy an existing product than to spend time creating a new product.

Determine restrictions/security issues related to the project request
The GIUL/GIMG needs to be aware of all project request constraints so that he/she can decide whom to assign as the GISP for the project, ensure security considerations are not breached, and can produce a product that meets all the necessary requirements.

PHASE 2: Project Assignment

So now you've received an assignment. What should you do next?
When you receive a project request from your manager, make sure you gather the necessary information. Your manager may also ask you to talk directly to the customer in order to gather additional information. You should ensure that, at the minimum, you:

- Clearly understand the assignment
- Know when the assignment needs to be completed

Certain high-priority projects will need to be completed immediately. Make sure you understand, and are able to meet, required deadlines. Managing customer expectations along with establishing time and resource requirements for production is a key step in defining a project's scope and effectively supporting the mission.

PHASE 3: Exploration – Data Collection

The next phase in the production process is exploration. This phase includes both data collection and initial data analysis.
You should begin collecting data as soon after receiving the project request as possible. Talk to your manager about existing resources and find out where to go to gather additional data. Your manager may redirect you to another section within FEMA, or ask you to interface directly with the customer.

You may find that data is already available from internal or external sources or that, in some cases it is not available and needs to be developed. In all cases, it is important to work with the customer to ensure that the data used is as accurate and current as possible.

PHASE 3: Exploration – Initial Data Analysis

During the initial data analysis, you will examine the data to determine the method to satisfy the customer's request.
When analyzing data, you should:

- Write down what you think the product should shows
- Describe what you are mapping (the data)
- Describe what the data tells you (the distribution)
- Note any special considerations such as outliers, high or low values, or missing values

PHASE 4: Production–Building the Product

The fourth phase, Production, involves building the product, conducting further analysis of the data, and conducting a review of the final product. This phase within the product development process is key to adding value to the visualization of geospatially-enabled data.

As you begin the production of a product, you should always consider the following:
- Symbology requirements
- Product layout standards
- Fulfillment of all requirements within the project request

Symbology
The standard symbology that should be used for all ICS-compliant documents and reporting structures is the FEMA standard ICS symbol-set as described in the FEMA Incident Action Planning Guide. This is especially true for Incident Maps that are included within Incident Action Plans (IAP), and other ICS-200-series forms.

(See FEMA Geospatial Incident Management and Support Guide.)

Standards
Your geospatial manager will provide direction about the standards you will be expected to meet. This may include standards for data use, disclaimers to include on maps, and general layout guidance. Your supervisor should also provide direction about Regional processes for organizing data, products and graphics. These Regional standards are often contained in Standard Operating Procedures (SOPs).

Phase 4: Production – Value-Added Analysis
Most analytic products should contain a brief synopsis that communicates the results, meaning and significance. This can be as simple as a few sentences, but should strive to eliminate any questions the customer might have about the overall story that the product was intended to convey. This will ensure a more efficient response. Usually, it is your manager's responsibility to include this synopsis, but sometimes it can also fall on your shoulders.

For products sent via email, this description can be the first few lines in the body of the message. For products posted to another dissemination platform, this can be included in a "Description" field about the product.

Phase 4: Production –Quality Assurance/Quality Control
Before you deliver a finished product to a customer, you should always have a member of your team review your work. While this does not have to be a formal quality assurance/quality control process, it is a critical part of the production process, since a fresh set of eyes can often find errors that may have been inadvertently overlooked during the production process.

Depending on the size of your team or the priority of the product, your reviewer may either be your supervisor or another GIS Specialist.

Quality assurance/Quality control
The goal of quality assurance/quality control is to improve development and test processes so that defects do not arise when the product is being developed. The goal of quality control (QC) is to identify defects after a product is developed, but before it is released.

Phase 4: Production –Provide Specific Feedback

In addition to making sure that all established standards and guidelines have been met, the quality assurance/quality control reviewer may also provide specific feedback about the product. This might include feedback as to whether the product:

- Conveys a clear story/the story you want to tell.
- Is based on current data and authoritative datasets.
- Includes data source references.
- Is visually appealing.

Remember that the products you produce should do more than just document information. Your ability to analyze and communicate data will enable other members of the team to more quickly and effectively support the disaster effort.

PHASE 5: Dissemination

The final phase in the production process is dissemination. As a GIS Specialist, you may or may not be responsible for the actual distribution of the products. If you are not, it is your responsibility to alert your supervisor once the product is completed so that they can then distribute the product to the customer.

GIU products can be provided in digital and/or hardcopy formats.

Digital
Products may be saved and disseminated in various digital formats, including PDF or common graphical formats (e.g. jpeg, gif, Tiff, png, etc.), and as tabular reports and summaries of data.

There are multiple ways to share information in these formats, including:

- Email
- Shared Drives
- File Transfer Protocols (FTPs)
- Information Sharing Platforms

Hardcopy
Physical products such as maps can also be provided in hardcopy format. After notification of completion of a production request, hardcopy products are often sent to the customer to close the loop on the request process.

Depending on the product requirements, hardcopy products may need to be put into one of the following formats before dissemination:

- Large format
- Map books

Lesson Summary

This lesson presented the following topics:

- Identify the GIS products that need to be produced during a disaster effort
- Recognize the GIS product workflow process
- Recognize the GIS quality assurance/quality control process

The next lesson explains how to work within the Unit.

Lesson 5: Working Within the Unit

Lesson Overview

In Lesson 4, you learned how to respond to common requests for GIS products and services. In this lesson, you will learn how to work within a GIS Unit (GIU). You will learn how geospatial products are compiled and analyzed and how metadata is used to document GIS data. You will also learn about dealing with the time constraints you will encounter when working in a GIU.

This lesson should take approximately 25 minutes to complete.

Learning Objectives

By the end of this lesson, you will be able to:

- Compile geospatial data into geospatial products
- Analyze data to support incident decision making

Identify how to document data

- Identify strategies for working within time constraints

Tying It Back to the Job

This lesson aligns with the following Position Task Book (PTB) Behaviors/Activities:

- Manage geospatial data
- Generate geospatial products
- Practice effective and appropriate interpersonal communication and team behavior

Importance of Geospatial Products

During an incident, the geospatial products you produce are used across all levels of FEMA to help decision-makers allocate and deploy resources in support of State and local partners and make the critical decisions needed to support the mission.

You are responsible for gathering the information needed to develop the requested products. Necessary information will come from a variety of sources and will be provided in diverse formats.

Data Gathering

Gathering timely and accurate data is a critical GIS task. During a disaster, you will be challenged to quickly gather and combine information to create products that can help emergency planners more effectively support the mission.

As a GISP, you will need to very quickly become familiar with the data sources available to you so that you can quickly access the information you need. You may even want to develop a checklist of available data sources that you can refer to as needed.

Compiling Geospatial Data to Create Products

Once you have the data you need, your next task is to compile the data into the geospatial products you have been asked to produce. Depending on the needs of your customer, you may be asked to provide products in the form of a map, a spreadsheet, a briefing slide, or even a written report.

Be sure to work closely with your customer to identify the type of product needed.

Data Layers for GIS

As you have already learned, the products that you will be asked to produce depend on the type of incident and the stage of the incident you are in. In some cases, you may need to compile multiple layers of data to create the product.

For example, in the event of a flood, emergency planners will want to know where the dry areas are located so that disaster facilities can be established. To meet this need, you may need to create maps showing flood extent layered with information about transportation networks and available facilities.

Data Analysis

Regardless of the complexity of the task, your goal is always to develop timely, accurate, and relevant geospatial information and products that can be easily interpreted by multiple end users for a wide range of disaster relief functions.

This means that you will do more than simply compile data. You also need to carefully analyze the data to ensure that the products you create give decision makers the information they need to make informed decisions.

Data Analysis and Incident Decision Making

Accurate and timely data analysis is critical in a disaster situation and can even result in lives saved.

Read the Story Data Analysis and Incident Decision Making

"The incident area is one of the most important situation products that the GIU can provide as it represents the areas where resources are directed to support the most severely impacted communities. Defining the incident area relies upon authoritative information from SMEs.

During Hurricane Ike, we received a NOAA SLOSH model indicating a completely inundated area that included Texas City, Beaumont and Galveston as well as the Bolivar peninsula. The evening prior to landfall, the FCO indicated that we were looking at an estimated 80-billion dollar event in which 40% of the population had not evacuated, resulting in a heavy ESF-9 US&R footprint. The need for the GIU to provide comprehensive information to definite the incident area was of paramount importance.

Over the next 72-hours post landfall, we coordinated closely with NOAA and the State to gradually refine the incident area and determined that certain key areas were not catastrophically impacted. While the SLOSH model from the NWS was the authoritative source, it no longer served as the best available information as it began to conflict with other information sources.

Further analysis showed that the SLOSH model had overestimated the impact area because the pixel resolution and vertical datum were not adjusted to include the seawalls and other control structures that were responsible for protecting both Texas City and Beaumont from the Storm surge.

Careful analysis enabled us to make the decision to refine and correct the incident area and to provide more accurate information for both a briefing for the President of the United States and for life-saving and life-sustaining operations support."
- As told by the FEMA GIU Leader for this disaster.

What is Metadata?

As a GISP, you are also responsible for creating metadata records for the data you develop. A metadata record represents the "who, what, when, where, why, and how" of a digital resource. It compiles information into a single record that captures the basic characteristics of your product and makes your product identifiable.

Metadata can be used to document common types of data, including GIS files, databases, and imagery.

Metadata Standards

The current Federal standard for geospatial data is the Content Standard for Digital Geospatial Metadata developed by the Federal Geographic Data Committee (FGDC). Whenever possible, full metadata for all new or event-specific data, GIS files or earth imagery should be created in compliance with these standards.

NOTE: Any data that will be made publicly available on the www.fema.gov site must have full metadata.

Metadata Minimum Elements

Sometimes, during the response to an incident, there is not sufficient time or resources to create fully compliant metadata records. For those times, metadata records must be created with the following minimum elements:
- Abstract
- Title
- Originator
- Publication Date
- Process Description
- Geographic Coordinate System Name
- Horizontal Datum Name

- Security Classification
- Time Period (Currency, Date and time)

The Nature of the Beast

As a GISP, you may find yourself working on multiple projects simultaneously. At any given time, you could be providing information about shelter or housing, responding to a request for information about urgently needed medical supplies, and gathering data about the location of logistics facilities.

Multi-tasking is a crucial skill that you will need as you work on diverse projects for different groups

Dealing with Tight Deadlines

When working within an incident, you are often required to produce geospatial products on a very tight timeline. To accomplish this, keep the following considerations in mind:
- Prioritize geospatial product requests
- Negotiate timelines for production
- Communicate realistic expectations
- Ask for additional resources if needed

Prioritize geospatial product requests

Not all geospatial products have the same level of priority. You should check with your supervisor (GIMG, GIUL, SITL or others) to determine which geospatial products are required most urgently, and begin working on those first.

Negotiate timelines for production

The customer may be unaware of your workload and may not understand the amount of time required to create a geospatial product. Do not hesitate to express your concerns about a deadline for a product with your customer and/or your supervisor when necessary.

Communicate realistic expectations

If products are needed on a short timeframe, there is bound to be a trade-off in terms of the quality of the product. Make sure you communicate this clearly with your supervisor and/or customer. Remember, having products created in a timely manner is sometimes more important than making them visually appealing with the best colors, symbology, etc. In general, if you have any issues that would prevent you from accomplishing the objective in a timely manner, you should communicate these issues as early in the process as possible.

Ask for additional resources if needed

If you feel overwhelmed and think it is not possible to complete all the geospatial products assigned to you, you should feel comfortable going to your supervisor to ask for additional resources. If other GISPs are not available, your supervisor may have suggestions for another solution.

Lesson Summary

This lesson presented the following topics:

- Compile geospatial data into map and data products
- Analyze data to support incident decision making
- Identify how to document data
- Identify strategies for working within time constraints

The next lesson will describe tactics for working with sensitive data.

Lesson 6: Working with Sensitive Data
Lesson Overview
In the previous lesson, you learned what it is like to work within a GIU. You learned how to compile data into maps and data products, how to analyze geospatial data to provide answers to diverse questions, how to document data and how to work within tight time constraints.

In this lesson, you will learn how to share, store, and protect the sensitive data you may encounter as part of your work. You will learn about requirements to adhere to copyright, disclaimer, licensing, and other sensitive product and data distribution protocols.
This lesson should take approximately 10 minutes to complete.

Learning Objectives
By the end of this lesson, you will be able to:
- Recognize how to work with sensitive data

Tying It Back to the Job
This lesson aligns with the following Position Task Book (PTB) Behavior/Activity:
- Comply with established policy and protocols

Using Markings and Disclaimers
When working in a GIU, you may sometimes encounter material that includes sensitive or personal information that needs to be protected. This lesson will introduce you to the common disclaimers used at FEMA to avoid the inadvertent disclosure of sensitive information.

Common disclaimers for products generated by the GIU include:
- Privacy Act Disclaimers
- For Official Use Only Disclaimers
- Disclaimers Requiring Coordination and Approval
- Commercial Imagery Markings

Privacy Act Disclaimer
The Privacy Act of 1974 provides protection against unauthorized disclosure of any records (documents, papers, charts, graphics, maps, etc.) which contain a person's name or other Personally-Identifiable Information (PII).

As a GISP, it is important to recognize that all data derived from the Individual Assistance (IA) program is protected under the Privacy Act, specifically when an individual applicant could be identified from the map.

Derived map products that include PII require a disclaimer that contains the following language:
This document may contain information protected under the Privacy Act of 1974, 5 U.S.C. §552a (2000). Neither this document nor the material contained therein may be reproduced, stored in a retrieval system or transmitted in any form or by any means without the prior permission of FEMA.

Protecting Personally Identifiable Information

One way to protect PII is to develop map products at a scale of 1:100,000 or greater. Most map products developed at this scale will not require the disclaimer presented on the previous screen, though this should be verified with the appropriate authorities including the IA Branch Director (IABD), and the Office of Chief Counsel (OCC) representative.

If such a scale is not possible, alternative presentations of the data should be used. This might include, for example creating a product that generalizes IA applicant data using the U.S. National Grid (USNG) at 1 kilometer intervals.

Recognizing Authoritative Data Sources

To preclude unauthorized access and ensure that all documents covered under the Privacy Act are handled appropriately, your manager will:
- Ensure that all PII are properly secured
- Ensure that any and all sensitive materials are destroyed using a cross-cut shredder

Properly Secured

Sensitive materials may be stored electronically as encrypted digital files or password-protected emails; printed copies may be stored in a locked file cabinet.

What is FOUO?

The marking, For Official Use Only (FOUO), is used to identify materials that contain unclassified information of a sensitive nature. While not classified, FOUO materials need to be protected in accordance with appropriate security policy.

FOUO designations require coordination with the data provider and approval through the Planning Section Chief and FCO. All maps, geospatial products, charts, and other graphics that meet this threshold are prominently marked in the upper right and lower left corners with the following caveat:
- Unclassified // For Official Use Only

For Official Use Only

According to FEMA policy, "FOUO" is a designation that applies to unclassified information of a sensitive nature, not otherwise categorized by statute or regulation. To further meet this definition, the unauthorized disclosure of such information must have the potential to adversely impact a person's privacy or welfare, the conduct of Federal programs, or other programs or operations essential to the national interest.

Products that contain addresses or phone numbers (such as maps, reports with the FCO's phone number and so on) are all examples of FOUO information.

Protected

FOUO materials require special handling. They should always be covered and marked appropriately. They cannot be shared or left out, and they cannot be downgraded. Unless approval is granted, FOUO materials should stay within the JFO at all times.

Disclaimers Requiring Coordination and Approval

Special issues at the JFO may require the use of other disclaimers included in the standard operating procedures. These are coordinated with your supervisor and program personnel who are involved with the final products. These are approved by the Office of Chief Counsel (OCC) representative. This often involves restrictions on distribution of map products to only authorized parties, or written designation on the geospatial product.

Such a product might include, for example, a disclaimer such as the following:
FOR INTERNAL USE ONLY: This product may be protected by one or more copyrights and license restrictions. Neither this document nor the material contained herein may be reproduced, stored in a retrieval system, or transmitted in any form or by any means without the prior written permission of the FEMA Federal Coordinating Officer.

Working with Commercial Imagery

As a GISP, you will also work with commercial imagery, most of which is licensed or copyrighted. When working with commercial imagery, you must convey the data license terms and conditions as appropriate.

Data License Information

It is also recommended that data license information be included when sharing/distributing image products. The format for marking products should adhere to the following template:
© 2007 "Vendor's Name"
Licensed under "Contract Name"
Note: If the copyright material is only part of the work, the notice should read: "Contains data © 2007 "Vendor's Name". For display purposes (such as when creating PowerPoint® slides, posters, etc.), you must maintain the "Copyright: © 2007 "Vendor's Name" marking.

Releasing Information to the Public

FEMA is making more and more information available to the public, not only through traditional news media, but through emergent social media platforms as well. This is also true for geospatial data and products.

Before releasing any geospatial products to the public, be sure the products have been approved for release by your supervisor.

Lesson Summary
This lesson presented the following topics:
* Recognize how to work with sensitive data

The next lesson explains how to use remote sensing products.

Lesson 7: Using Remote Sensing Products
Lesson Overview
This lesson will focus on remote sensing capabilities and the use of remote sensing products in GIS.

This lesson should take approximately 10 minutes to complete.

Learning Objectives
By the end of this lesson, you will be able to:
- Identify remote sensing capabilities
- Recognize the steps of the remote sensing workflow process
- Use FEMA damage classification system to convey the severity of an incident

Tying It Back to the Job
This lesson aligns with the following PTB Behavior/Activity:
- Manage geospatial data

What is Remote Sensing?
Remote sensing (RS) refers to the acquisition of information (typically imagery) from ground, aerial, or satellite sensors.

RS is very useful during an event when areas are isolated or communication is limited. RS can provide critical information about an event, which can then be integrated into geographic information systems to produce maps or analytic databases.
This information can then be used by emergency managers and decision makers at all levels of the response structure.

How is Remote Sensing Used?
Remote sensing capabilities greatly improve a geospatial information unit's ability to provide situational awareness for a wide area in a very short timeframe.
Imagery and the data derived from it can be used to:
- Assess levels/patterns of damage within disaster areas.
- Assess impacts to populations and critical infrastructure.
- Monitor and assess the extent of flood inundation and storm surge extents.
- Assess scope and extent of debris fields within an area of impact (AOI).
- Support Situation Awareness in inaccessible areas.
- Quickly assess the order of magnitude of an incident.
- Enhance communication with survivors about the status of property and infrastructure.

How are Remote Sensing Efforts Coordinated?
To help coordinate remote sensing efforts, the Interagency Remote Sensing Coordination Cell (IRSCC) was established.

The mission of the IRSCC is to improve the governance of Federal remote sensing operations, which in turn helps decision makers make better and faster decisions by providing them with a more thorough understanding of the environment in which they operate.

The IRSCC accomplishes this through a combination of personnel, organization, technology, training, and processes.

Remote Sensing Capabilities

In your role as GIS Specialist, you will analyze data and images gathered by remote sensing sensor capabilities attached to platforms (e.g., satellites, planes and ground vehicles) that can observe areas of interest (AOI).

To gather the information needed (and account for differing environmental factors), a number of different capabilities may be used.

- Panchromatic Imagery
- Multispectral Imagery (MSI)
- Hyperspectral Imagery (HSI)
- Oblique Imagery
- Infrared Radiation (IR)
- RADAR
- LiDAR

Panchromatic Imagery

Panchromatic images are literal representations of objects or terrain derived from capturing reflected visible light by means of a panchromatic system. Unlike photography it does not use chemically processed film and therefore may be available on a Near Real-Time (NRT) basis. Panchromatic imagery can be obtained from satellites, aircraft, or unmanned aerial systems (UAS).

Projected uses for panchromatic imagery include:
- Assessing levels and patterns of damage within disaster areas
- Assessing scope and extent of debris fields within disaster areas
- Monitoring and assessing the extent of flooding

Multispectral Imagery

Multispectral remote sensing is the process of simultaneously measuring reflected or emitted energy across a variety of relatively narrow spectral bands, ranging from ultraviolet to the thermal-infrared portion of the electromagnetic spectrum.

Projected uses include:
- Analyzing changes to an area before and after an event (also known as 'change detection')
- Detecting pollution in or toxic contamination of water and soil
- Assessing the impact of drought on agriculture
- Providing a broad indication of flood inundation

Hyperspectral Imagery

Hyperspectral imaging is the process of scanning and displaying an image within a section of the electromagnetic spectrum. To create an image the eye can see, the energy levels of a target are color-coded and then mapped in layers. This set of images provides specific information about the way an object transmits, reflects, or absorbs energy in various wavelengths. Using this procedure, the unique signature can reveal valuable information otherwise undetectable by the human eye, such as fingerprints or contamination of groundwater or food.

Projected uses include:
- Detecting pollution in or toxic contamination of water and soil
- Assessing the impact of drought on agriculture

Oblique Imagery

Oblique imagery is aerial photography – taken by a low-flying aircraft equipped with a five camera system – that is captured at approximately a 45 degree with the ground. This allows viewers to see and measure the sides of objects, in addition to the tops. Oblique imagery more closely resembles how people typically view their landscape as opposed to orthogonal images, which are overhead photos from a long-range satellite. Oblique imagery has the ability to measure water marks of each point it photographs.

Projected uses include:
- For major events, oblique imagery provides additional details about damaged areas and may help to identify damage to buildings.
- Post-event oblique imagery can help identify collapsed and damaged buildings where traditional "top-down" imagery will only show rooftops.

Infrared Radiation

Infrared radiation is electromagnetic energy just below the visible light spectrum. Infrared remote sensing instruments function by sensing infrared radiation (IR) that is naturally emitted or reflected by the Earth's surface or from the atmosphere, or by sensing signals transmitted from, and reflected back to, a satellite or aircraft. Since thermal IR data are based on temperatures rather than visible radiation, the data may be obtained day or night.

Projected uses include:
- Determining forest fire or wildfire boundaries, or spot fire flare-ups
- Assessing damage to vegetation from various hazards
- Assisting in non-urban search and rescue activities

RADAR

Radar, which stands for RAdio Detection And Ranging, is a method of sending and receiving electromagnetic waves to determine the range of remote objects through measurement of the returned signals. Radar imaging provides the ability to detect objects at distances where sound or visible light emissions would be weak or non-existent.

Projected uses Include:
- Determination of flood extents
- Identifying changes to terrain and land surface
- Identification of oil spills on water.
- This data is especially useful in combination with comparable pre-event data of this type.

LiDAR

Light Detection and Ranging (LiDAR) works something like Radar, but instead of transmitting radio waves, LiDAR transmits laser light pulses. The light bounces off objects and scatters. A telescope receives the backscattered light and a detector measures the intensity. Using the data, a computer produces a precise 3D image. LiDAR instruments can operate as profilers and as scanners, day and night. LiDAR can also serve as a ranging device to determine altitudes (topography mapping) and depths (in water).

Airborne LIDAR is very useful during an event because it can be used to measure heights of objects and features on the ground more accurately than with radar technology.

Projected uses include:
- Detecting small changes in land surface
- Detailed 3D modeling of land and structures
- Detecting near shore changes in bathymetry

This data is especially useful in combination with comparable pre-event data of this type.

Geo-Tagged Photos

While satellites and planes are a valuable resource for gathering data remotely, today they are no longer the only tools available. Smartphones can also be used to access geospatial data. With the increased availability of "smartphones" and GPS enabled digital cameras, emergency management personal can now provide critical information on developing situations in near-real time.

In addition, the aggregation of these photos (for example in social media outlets) can provide additional perspective on the "where and when" of developing situations.

Geospatial data

Geo-Tagged photos contain reference information, usually geographic coordinates (latitude and longitude) that indicate the location of the image. These photos can be collected easily and displayed immediately in situational awareness viewers to provide information about specific events.

360° Interactive Video

360° interactive video is also used to provide needed GIS information. This technology stitches photographs together to provide the end user with a unique virtual experience. Many users are now familiar with this process, in part thanks to Google's Street View© or Microsoft's Street Side©.

This imagery can be quickly collected with specialized equipment mounted on automobile roofs and processed immediately following collection. Processed imagery can be posted and available for use in most mapping applications shortly following acquisition.

Full-Motion Video (FMV)

Another technology used to provide GIS information is full-motion video (FMV). FMV provides the ability to view motion imagery dynamically in real-time (RT) or near-real time (NRT).

The continuous and persistent NRT capability of the feed enables users to view changes over time to the same target area. In addition, FMV can be simultaneously broadcast to multiple consumers, allowing all echelons (HQ, Regional, Field, State, etc.) to view the same picture at the same time.

Accessing RS Data

With proper coordination, RS data can be available to any user to assist with mission support requirements. For Stafford Act events, RS efforts are coordinated by FEMA through the JFO, RRCC, and NRCC RS Coordinators.

As the ESF 5 Coordinator, FEMA works with the US Geological Survey (USGS), National Geospatial Intelligence Agency (NGA), Department of Homeland Security (DHS), and other Federal departments and agencies. Imagery is acquired, analyzed, and disseminated using a systematic process referred to as TCPED that includes five phases: tasking, collection, processing, exploitation, and dissemination.

Collection Management

When working with remote sensing data, you will follow the TCPED framework shown here.

Tasking

The tasking phase of the project production process begins with the receipt of a GIS request. This request is received directly by the GIUL for large incidents or the GIMG for smaller incidents. The request may be submitted in either hardcopy or electronic format. The responsibility for tasking can be left to the GIUL at the Incident-level when assets are locally available and the expenditures have been approved and justified through the chain of command; however, most large and medium scale disasters will require extensive coordination with the Region and the HQ Remote Sensing Coordinator.

The determination of the area of interest (AOI) for collections is based on support requirements identified through the Joint Incident Objectives and Priorities set by the Unified Coordination Group. While it is safe to assume that adjacent areas will be included, requests for imagery should be very specific in coverage area and identify specific targets.

Collection

Once preliminary tasking is completed, the collection phase begins. This phase focuses on the acquisition of "raw" imagery. Because the post-event environment is dynamic, tasking and collection are closely linked; the combined tasks are reliant on continuous feedback.

Processing

During this phase, acquired imagery is processed. The processing requirements can include image registration, rectification, color balancing, and others. Once complete, the imagery is available for exploitation and dissemination.

Processing is often the most time-consuming, technically challenging, and resource-intensive process within the remote sensing lifecycle. Therefore, users in the Field are urged to rely on organizations with higher end workstations, broader bandwidth network infrastructure, and dedicated staff with reach back capabilities.

Several platforms exist, especially within the Department of Defense (DoD), which can assist FEMA personnel with the rapid receipt and processing of geospatial data, imagery, and other media.

Exploitation

This phase provides the interpretation required to generate usable end products. Analysis may be automated or interpreted visually by imagery analysts to derive vector data from the imagery source data. This derived data can then be attributed with key pieces of information to add value.

Dissemination

The final phase of the process ensures that the imagery and derived products are effectively delivered and available to the end users and products. This may be accomplished through a person-to-person exchange of physical media, embedded into a map viewer, or passed through email or web-based tools.

FEMA Damage Classification System

During an incident, RS data and imagery are analyzed and annotated based on the damage classification system guidelines developed by FEMA.

These guidelines are used by geospatial analysts to determine the type and magnitude of damage. Trained image analysts, including staff from NGA, delineate the damaged areas according to FEMA's criteria and provide this information to responders in both map and data product formats.

Lesson Summary

This lesson presented the following topics:

- Remote sensing capabilities
- The remote sensing workflow process
- FEMA Damage classification system

The next lesson explains how to check out of an incident.

Lesson 8: Checking out of an Incident
Lesson Overview
In Lesson 7, you learned how to work with remote sensing products. In this lesson, you will learn how to transition duties to a replacement and how to check out of an incident.
This lesson should take approximately 10 minutes to complete.

Learning Objectives
By the end of this lesson, you will be able to:
- Recognize how to transition responsibilities to incoming/replacement GIS staff
- Recognize how to check out of an incident

Tying It Back to the Job
This lesson aligns with the following PTB Behaviors/Activities:
- Ensure continuity of operations during the transition of duties to a replacement
- Properly check out of the incident

Leaving an Incident
Depending upon the incident objectives and the severity and stage of the incident, the GIU will both expand and contract as required. The goal is to ensure that the number of personnel available matches the needs of the mission.
As a GISP, you may find yourself leaving an incident under one of two circumstances:
- Transition to a replacement
- Incident closeout

Transition to replacement
Transition occurs when the incident is ongoing, but you are no longer able to remain at the JFO. When this happens, you must pass on your duties to a replacement staff member.

Incident closeout
Incident closeout occurs when the incident is concluding or the JFO is closing. When this happens, you are responsible for ensuring that all assigned GISP tasks are completed.

GISP Transition Responsibilities
As a GISP, some of your major responsibilities during transition are to:
- Document responsibilities and tasks
- Update products to ensure they are:
  - Useable
  - Accurate
  - Professional
- Archive all files
- Brief replacement staff

Document responsibilities and tasks

It is a best practice to provide a written summary that describes daily tasks and the status of all tasks, as well as specialized work processes and tools that may have been developed to streamline analysis. You should also document data workflows and GISP responsibilities for the replacement GISP. This will allow the replacement GISP to get up-to-speed quickly and ensure a smooth transition.

Useable

Ensure that source data is included and files are saved in a format that is universally accessible.

Accurate

Ensure documents have been updated regularly and cross-checked with authoritative sources.

Professional

Ensure that standards have been maintained and symbology and templates follow the FEMA conventions.

Archive all files

Ensure all files are saved electronically in logical order. This will avoid confusion once the replacement GISP takes over responsibilities.

Brief replacement staff

In order to ensure that replacement staff is appropriately set up to carry out their duties, it is critical that there is some time overlap between incoming personnel and personnel who are transitioning out. To ensure that duties are handed over smoothly, this time overlap should ideally be one to two days.

GISP Incident Checkout Responsibilities

Once the GIU closes down at the direction of the Planning Section Chief or at the closure of the JFO, staff members will need to check out. As a GISP, you have responsibilities for completing the check out process. Some of your major responsibilities include:

- Complete the Demobilization Checkout Form
- Obtain a performance appraisal
- Return all equipment
- Check out of the Automated Deployment Database
- Submit final documents

Complete the Demobilization Checkout Form

A Demobilization Checkout Form is required for all staff checking out of JFOs.

Obtain a performance appraisal

Your performance appraisal will be handled by your supervisor. He/she will evaluate and document your performance for an assignment.

Return all equipment

You will need to check out with the Accountable Property Manager (APM) in order to return job-related equipment such as:

- Laptop and specialized GIS hardware and software
- Cellular phone (if applicable)
- Handheld GPS (if applicable)
- Camera (if applicable)
- Air Card (if applicable)

Check out of the Automated Deployment Database (ADD)

To check out of the Automated Deployment Database (ADD), you will need the following information:

- Date of checkout
- Releasing official

Submit final documents

Final documents to be submitted include:

- Timesheet
- Appraisal form
- Travel voucher

Lesson Summary

This lesson presented the following topics:

- Recognize how to transition responsibilities to incoming/replacement GIS staff
- Recognize how to check out of an incident

The next lesson summarizes the course and provides a review of the main points covered in this course.

Lesson 9: Summary and Conclusion
Lesson Overview
This lesson provides a brief summary of the GIS Specialist course. After reviewing the summary, you will receive instructions for taking the course post-test.

This lesson should take approximately 5 minutes to complete.

Lesson 2: Key Points
Lesson 2 provided information about the resources and processes you will use as a GISP and reviewed the different components of the ICS organization and the GIS Unit, identified key geospatial doctrine, and identified various geospatial systems, tools, and data sources.

The objectives for this lesson were:
- Recognize how GIS supports other components in a JFO
- Identify key geospatial doctrine and materials
- Identify FEMA geospatial systems and tools
- Recognize authoritative data sources

Lesson 3: Key Points
Lesson 3 focused on the initial actions, tools, and materials necessary when getting started at the Joint Field Office. It also provided an overview of the kinds of geospatial products you will be expected to produce.

The objectives for this lesson were:
- Recognize how to check in to a Joint Field Office
- Identify how to gather information relevant to an assignment
- Identify the types of geospatial products that need to be produced during a disaster

Lesson 4: Key Points
Lesson 4 summarized the geospatial products you will be asked to produce and provided an overview of the workflow process you will follow as you produce these products. It also provided an overview of the quality assurance/quality control process used to ensure the production of high quality geospatial products.

The objectives for this lesson were:
- Identify the geospatial products commonly produced during an incident
- Recognize the geospatial product workflow process
- Recognize the quality assurance/quality control process used to ensure the quality of geospatial products

Lesson 5: Key Points
In Lesson 5, you learned how to work within a GIS Unit (GIU) including how geospatial products are compiled and analyzed and how metadata is used to document geospatial data. You also learned about dealing with the time constraints that you will encounter when working in a GIU.

The objectives for this lesson were:
- Compile geospatial data into map and data products
- Analyze data to support incident decision making

- Identify how to document data
- Identify strategies for working within time constraints

Lesson 6: Key Points

In Lesson 6, you learned how to work with sensitive data including what sensitive data includes, what markings and disclaimers are used, and how to correctly work with, share, and store products that include sensitive data. You also learned how to adhere to requirements associated with the use of copyright and licensed data.
The objectives for this lesson were:

- Recognize how to work with sensitive data

Lesson 7: Key Points

In Lesson 7, you focused on the use of remote sensing products in GIS.
The objectives for this lesson were:

- Identify remote sensing capabilities
- Recognize the steps of the remote sensing workflow process
- Use FEMA Damage Classifications to convey the severity of an incident

Lesson 8: Key Points

In Lesson 8, you learned how to transition duties to a replacement and how to check out of an incident.
The objectives for this lesson were:

- Recognize how to transition responsibilities to incoming/replacement GIS staff
- Recognize how to check out of an incident

Additional EMI Independent Study Courses

To learn more about the content covered during this course, you can take additional EMI independent study courses such as:
Introduction to GIS courses (provided by many external sources)

- EMI (E190) ArcGIS for Emergency Managers
- ESRI – Learning ArcGIS Desktop
- ESRI – HAZUS-MH online courses
- ESRI – Learning ArcGIS Spatial Analyst
- ESRI – Creating, Editing and Managing Geodatabases for ArcGIS Desktop
- ESRI – Understanding GIS Queries
- ESRI – Using Python in ArcGIS Desktop – Introduction to Python and Integration with ArcGIS Desktop
- ESRI – Basics of the Geodatabase Data Model

Online Resources

For more information, you can also log onto these websites:

- FEMA Doctrine: https://www.fema.gov/policies
- Content Standards for Digital Geospatial Metadata:http://www.fgdc.gov/metadata/csdgm/
- GIS Dictionary: http://support.esri.com/en/knowledgebase/GISDictionary/browse/